D0229295

RUSSIA AND MOSCOW

PHILIP STEELE

W

FRANKLIN WATTS
LONDON • SYDNEY

DEVELOPING WORLD

RUSSIA AND MOSCOW

W
FRANKLIN WATTS
LONDON · SYDNEY

First published in 2013 by
Franklin Watts
338 Euston Road
London
NW1 3BH

Franklin Watts Australia
Level 17/207 Kent Street
Sydney
NSW 2000

Copyright © Franklin Watts 2013

HB ISBN 978 1 4451 2362 2
Library eBook ISBN 978 14451 2368 4

Dewey number: 947'.0863
A CIP catalogue record for this book is
available from the British Library.

Series Editor: Julia Bird
Series Advisor: Emma Epsley, geography teacher and consultant
Series Design: sprout.uk.com

Picture credits:

Olga A/Shutterstock: 31t. Bryan & Cherry Alexander/Arctic Photo: 11. Goran Bogicevic/Shutterstock: 9b. Cescassawin/
Dreamstime: front cover b, 3b. Danilov/Shutterstock: 27bl.Dmitry Ersler/Shutterstock: 28. Jack F/Dreamstime: 19b. Alexei
Fateev/Alamy: 12. Iakov Filimonov/Shutterstock: 6b. Sue Flood/Getty Images: 23. Oleg Fokin/Shutterstock: 7b.
FotograFF/Shutterstock: 20. Anton Gvozdokov/Shutterstock: 13cl, 13cr. ID1974/Shutterstock: 17t. ITAR-TASS/Alamy: 14,
41,43t. Julia 161/Dreamstime: 26, 39tr. Martti Kainulainen/Rex Features: 19t. Peter Kirilov/Shutterstock: 35b. Pavel L Photo
and Video/Shutterstock: front cover t, 3t, 10t, 30. Pavel Losevsky/Dreamstime: 33b. Ludovic Maisant/Corbis: 38.
Anna Martynova/Dreamstime: 15. Ian Masterton/Alamy: 33t. Michael Nicholson/Corbis: 8b. Nordroden/Dreamstime: 24.
Oledjio/Shutterstock: 18. Olemac/Shutterstock: 43b. Sergey Petrov/Shutterstock: 34. PhotoXpress/Zuma Press/Alamy: 27t.
Ekaterina Pokrovsky/Dreamstime: 36. Valeriya Popova/Shutterstock: 13b. Prysha/Dreamstime: 37. RIA/Novosti/Alamy: 27br.
RIA/Novosti/Topfoto: 39tl. rm/Shutterstock: 40. Andrey Rudakov/Bloomberg/Getty Images: 16. Shamuker Rusian/Photo-
shot: 31b. Mircea Preda Struteanu/Dreamstime: 22. Toxawww/Dreamstime: 39bl. Raluca Tudor/Dreamstime: 32. Vadiuhaps/
Shutterstock: 17t. Vasily Vishnevskiy/Dreamstime: 25. VLADJ55/Shutterstock: 13t. Lilyana Vynogradova/
Shutterstock: 39br. Westend6/Gmbh/Alamy: 42. withGod/Shutterstock: 21b. Yuri4u80/Dreamstime: 9t. yykkaa/Shutter-
stock: 21t. Zuma Press/Alamy: 29, 35t.

Every effort has been made by the Publishers to ensure that the websites on page 45 of this book are suitable
for children, and that they contain no inappropriate or offensive material. However, because of the nature of
the Internet, it is impossible to guarantee that the contents of these sites will not be altered. We strongly advise
that Internet access is supervised by a responsible adult.

Printed in Malaysia

Franklin Watts is a division of
Hachette Children's Books,
an Hachette UK company.
www.hachette.co.uk

DEVELOPING WORLD

RUSSIA AND MOSCOW

CONTENTS

THE NEW RUSSIA

It is 25th May, and Russian teenagers are celebrating 'the Last Bell', the end of their final term at school. The boys dress in smart suits and the girls in formal black dresses, wearing sashes and lacy ribbons in their hair. There are presentations to teachers, speeches, laughter and tears.

CHILDREN OF CHANGE

When today's teenagers leave school, they face a very different future from their parents and grandparents. In the last hundred years Russia has experienced rule by an emperor, two world wars, revolutions, civil war, communism and capitalism. Even the national borders have altered. Great social and economic changes have swept across the land. Russia today is more prosperous than at any time in its history. But what kind of nation has it become, and how would today's teenagers like it to be in the future?

A GIANT NATION

Russia occupies about one-eighth of the planet's surface, so what happens there affects almost every part of the world. It is the biggest nation on Earth, with an area of 17,098,242 sq km – about 1.8 times the size of the USA. Bleak, deep-frozen tundra borders Russia's Arctic coast, while further south are great forests, known as taiga. In the far south, grassy steppes are bordered by high mountains. Russian summers can be warm and sunny, but the winters are snowy and bitterly cold.

FROM EUROPE TO ASIA

The Russian Federation covers nine time zones and straddles two continents. European Russia occupies the vast plain which stretches from Central Europe to the Ural mountains. In the south are the Caucasus mountains and the coasts of the Black Sea and the Caspian Sea. Elbrus is Europe's highest mountain peak, soaring to 5,642 metres. Asian Russia extends all the way from the Urals to the volcanoes of the Pacific rim. This region of plains and plateaus is known as Siberia. It is crossed by three of the ten longest rivers in the world: the Yenisey, Ob-Irtysh and Amur. Baikal is world's deepest lake, and may hold as much as 20 per cent of the world's fresh water.

NORWAY
FINLAND
KALININGRAD ESTONIA
LATVIA
St Petersburg
BELARUS
Moscow
Nizhny Novogorod
UKRAINE
Kazan
Don River
Volga River
Sea of Azov
Rostov-na-Donu
Samara
Black Sea
Volgograd
CAUCASUS MTS
MT. ELBRUS (5,642m)
GEORGIA
Caspian Sea
AZERBAIJAN

School leavers in the city of Vladimir line up for the 'Last Bell' ceremony.

WRANGEL ISLAND

● Anadyr

Arctic Ocean

East Siberian Sea

Barents Sea

● Murmansk

Laptev Sea

KOLYMA MTS

Bering Sea

Kara Sea

CHERSKIY MTS

KAMCHATKA PENINSULA

● Arkhangel'sk

S I B E R I A

● Okhotsk

Sea of Okhotsk

Yenisey River

● Yakutsk

URAL MOUNTAINS

Anagara River

● Kirov

R U S S I A N   F E D E R A T I O N

SAKHALIN ISLAND

● Perm

Ob River

Lena River

Irtysh River

● Ufa ● Yekaterinburg

Amur River

● Khabarovsk

● Tomsk

● Omsk

● Krasnoyarsk

● Novosibirsk

LAKE BAIKAL

Irkutsk ●

KAZAKHSTAN

● Vladivostok

MONGOLIA

CHINA

Sea of Japan

JAPAN

NORTH
KOREA

SPOTLIGHT ON RUSSIA

Yugyd Va national park is Russia's largest. It takes in some of the Ural mountains, which divide Europe from Asia.

FULL NAME: The Russian Federation

• SHORT NAME: Russia • AREA: 17,098,242 sq km • POPULATION: 143.3 million

• CAPITAL: Moscow (10.5 million)

• SECOND CITY: St Petersburg (4.8 million)

• LONGEST RIVER: Yenisey (5,539 km)

• HIGHEST MOUNTAIN: Elbrus (5,633 m)

• RESOURCES: Oil, natural gas, coal, gold, iron ore, chromium, nickel, copper, tin, lead, phosphates, timber, fish

PEOPLE AND NATION

BIG HISTORY

In 2012 President Vladimir Putin made a speech about Russia's future. He called on people to seek guidance from their country's past. Russia's eventful history certainly offers many lessons.

THE AGE OF EMPIRE

Russia's story begins in the Middle Ages (5–15th centuries CE), when a patchwork of cities and small states grew up in the lands of the Eastern Slavs. Over time the most powerful city became Moscow, capital of Muscovy. Its rulers forged all Russia into a single empire. Over the centuries this empire expanded westwards, southwards and eastwards across Siberia. Many of Russia's emperors or tsars were harsh rulers. While other European peoples were gaining more rights and freedoms, Russia's peasants remained serfs.

REVOLUTION AND CIVIL WAR

Revolutions broke out in 1905 and in 1917, during the First World War. A group called the Bolsheviks, led by Vladimir Ilyich Lenin, seized power. They founded the Russian Communist Party, which aimed to give power to the workers. The ruling tsar, Nicholas II, was shot in 1918. In a civil war that lasted until 1922, the communist Red Army defeated their opponents, who were known as the Whites. A new state was formed, the Union of Soviet Socialist Republics (USSR, or Soviet Union).

Lenin (1870–1924)
was a revolutionary.
His ideas influenced
world politics throughout
the 20th century.

Joseph Dzhugashvili, or 'Stalin' (1878–1953) was a ruthless, dictatorial leader.

COLD WAR AND REFORM

After the war, Soviet power dominated Eastern Europe. From 1945 to 1991 there was a Cold War, a period of tension between the USSR on one side and the USA and Western Europe on the other.

Political reform followed Stalin's death in 1953, but it was not until Mikhail Gorbachev was in power (1985–91) that the USSR really began to change. Gorbachev's aims included *perestroika* (re-structuring the system) and *glasnost* (openness), and relations with the West began to thaw. In 1991, a conservative group within the Communist Party tried to force Gorbachev from power. They failed, but the USSR collapsed. Fourteen regions broke away to become independent nations. The new Russian Federation was born, with a multi-party political system and a capitalist economy.

During the Cold War, both sides armed themselves with nuclear weapons and developed rocket technology.

STALIN'S RUSSIA

Lenin died in 1924. A cunning politician called Joseph Stalin soon won control. He pushed through reforms in industry and farming, but at great human cost. Millions of people died in a famine in 1932–33. Many people were murdered or sent to grim labour camps. At the start of the Second World War in 1939 Russia and Germany agreed not to attack each other, but in 1940 Adolf Hitler ordered the invasion of the USSR. The extraordinary Russian resistance and counter-attack was crucial to Germany's defeat in 1945. This 'Great Patriotic War' is still commemorated across Russia every 9th May.

MEET THE PEOPLE

504 538 539

As you travel across Russia, the forests seem to stretch on forever. Where are all the people? The population density is one of the lowest in the world, with just 8.4 people per square kilometre.

Russians buy fresh food at a local market in Preobrazhensky in Moscow.

THE RUSSIANS

Русские – pronounced *Russkiye*, means the Russians. The Russian language is written in a script named Cyrillic. Ethnic Russians, a Slavic people from European Russia, make up about 80 per cent of the national population. Over the ages they have also settled in many other parts of the former Russian empire and the USSR, as well as overseas.

HARSH TERRAIN

Russia may be the world's largest country, but its population of 143.3 million is barely 11 per cent of that in neighbouring China. One reason for this is the difficulty of making a home in Russia's harsher regions. In Siberia, winter temperatures can plunge to –60°C and permafrost makes the deeper soil as hard as iron. Eight out of ten Russians live in the west, where the land is better for farming and big cities are thriving.

UNITED OR DIVIDED?

In some parts of the country, non-Russians outnumber ethnic Russians. These regions are referred to as republics. Here, local languages may be used alongside Russian for schooling and government. The law guarantees the rights of minorities. In practice, ethnic tensions are quite common. Some of Russia's minorities have experienced centuries of conquest or resettlement and racism, and some old grievances have been stirred up since the break up of the old Soviet Union.

CHECHEN WAR

After the Soviet Union collapsed in 1991, the people of Chechnya demanded independence, as did many bordering regions. The government refused and sent in the army in a campaign against Chechen guerrillas and civilians. A brutal Second Chechen War began in 1999 and lasted ten years. This led to terrorist attacks by Chechens in Russian cities. Today the war is over, but it has left lasting bitterness.

PART OF THE WHOLE

Many other peoples live in the Russian Federation, comprising over 180 ethnic groups in all. Ukrainians, who are Slavs like the Russians, make up about two per cent of the national population. Turkic peoples such as the Tatars, Bashkir and Chuvash account for over six per cent. Most of these minority peoples lead much the same kind of lives as ethnic Russians, but in the Arctic some small groups, such as the Nenets and Sami, work to keep up their own traditions, herding reindeer or hunting and fishing for a living.

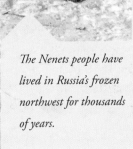

The Nenets people have lived in Russia's frozen northwest for thousands of years.

11

FOCUS ON: MOSCOW

SEASONAL CITY

People who live in Moscow (Moskva) are called Muscovites. Their city changes dramatically with the seasons. In the heat of summer, people can stroll or sun themselves in the leafy parks. In the snowy winter months pedestrians need to wrap up warm and wear furry or woollen hats, while traffic slithers over the ice and slush.

RUSSIA'S BIGGEST CITY

Moscow is the power-house of the Russian Federation. It is the capital city, the hub of political power, a centre of business and industry. It is by far the biggest city, too, with a population of over 10.5 million.

THE KREMLIN

At the heart of Moscow is the Kremlin, a medieval stronghold beside the Moscow River. Within its red walls are the golden domes of cathedrals, the tombs of the tsars, palaces, treasure houses, government buildings and the official residence of the President. Flanking the Kremlin is the wide open expanse of Red Square, used for grand military parades, concerts and many national events.

BUILDINGS

Ring roads divide the city into zones. Some architecture dates back to the time of the tsars, and many public buildings were built when Stalin was still in power. Grand railway terminals sit side by side with dreary high-rise housing blocks and factories from the 1960s and 70s. Glassy skyscrapers have shot up in recent years.

WEEKEND HOMES

Many of Moscow's super-rich own luxurious country houses, or *dachas*, in the forests around Moscow. Less wealthy city-dwellers also have their own dachas – shacks, summer houses and small cottages with vegetable plots outside the city limits. They are intended for recreation only, but these days some Muscovites move into them, renting out their city flats to make more money.

Snow is cleared from Red Square, beside St Basil's cathedral. About 15,000 snowploughs and trucks clear the streets during Moscow's long, fierce winters.

Moscow's Kremlin has been at the centre of Russian history for centuries.

The changing of the guard takes place at the Tomb of the Unknown Soldier. An eternal flame commemorates the troops who died in the 'Great Patriotic War' (see page 9).

Moscow's new business district overlooks the wide Moscow River.

Arbat Street is one of the oldest in Moscow. It is popular with tourists, who enjoy its hustle and bustle, its souvenir and antique shops, its buskers, street artists and fast food stalls.

POLITICS AND POWER

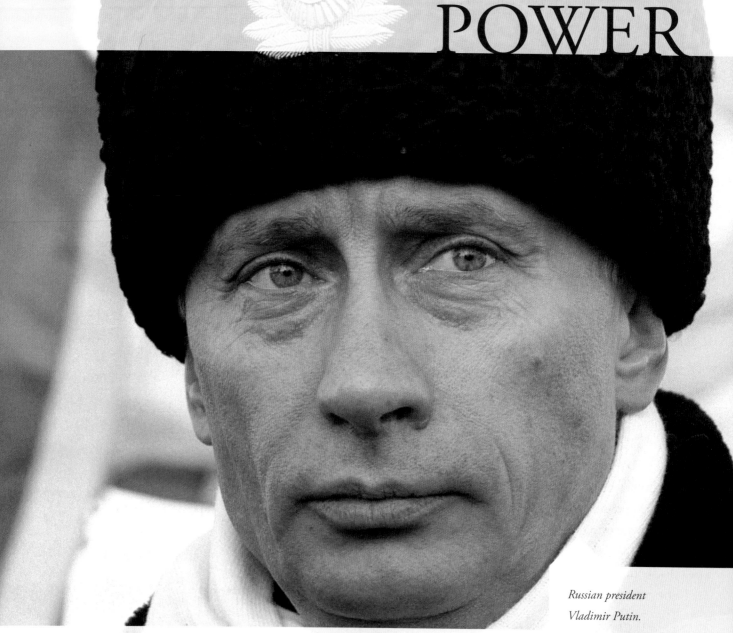

*Russian president
Vladimir Putin.*

The politics of today's Russia has been mainly shaped by two men, Boris Yeltsin and Vladimir Putin.

TIME OF TRANSITION

Boris Yeltsin was the elected president from 1991 to 1999, a chaotic period of great political change in Russia. Yeltsin took on great personal powers, even sending in tanks to attack the Russian parliament in 1993. His shock economic reforms deprived millions of people of the basic welfare which had been provided by the Soviet state. On the other hand, a few people became extremely rich and powerful, and were nicknamed oligarchs (members of a ruling elite). Crime and corruption flourished during this time.

PUTIN'S RUSSIA

Vladimir Putin, a former secret police chief, followed Yeltsin as president from 2001 to 2008. From 2008 to 2012 Putin swapped jobs with his prime minister Dmitry Medvedev, before being re-elected to the presidency in 2012. Under President Putin, the Russian economy has improved and stabilised. This has brought him widespread support. Putin is seen as a tough guy who gets things done and stands up for Russia in international politics. He is fond of public relations stunts and likes to present himself as a heroic man of action.

CRITICS

Putin's critics see him as an authoritarian leader, who likes to intimidate opponents and clamp down on protest. They accuse him of fixing elections and of failing to tackle corruption. There is a great gap between rich and poor, and oligarchs can still remain extremely wealthy – unless they fall out with Putin. Many now complain that Putin has too much personal power, and protests are growing.

HOW IT WORKS

Russia's president is head of state, while its prime minister heads the government. The Federal Assembly's upper house is called the Federation Council. It has two delegates from each of Russia's 83 provinces, regions and federal cities. The lower house is the State Duma, or parliament, whose 450 deputies are elected for five-year terms.

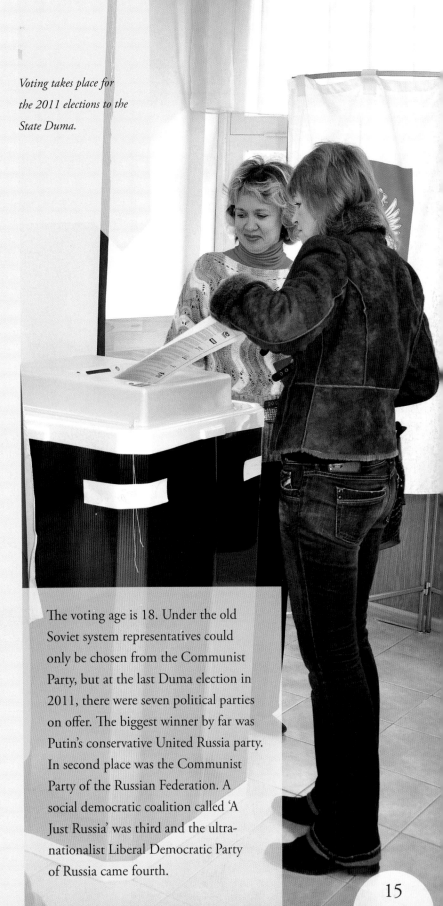

Voting takes place for the 2011 elections to the State Duma.

The voting age is 18. Under the old Soviet system representatives could only be chosen from the Communist Party, but at the last Duma election in 2011, there were seven political parties on offer. The biggest winner by far was Putin's conservative United Russia party. In second place was the Communist Party of the Russian Federation. A social democratic coalition called 'A Just Russia' was third and the ultra-nationalist Liberal Democratic Party of Russia came fourth.

MONEY MATTERS

Workers come off shift at the Sibirginsky mine in Siberia. This opencast pit supplies coal for the steel industry.

Back in 1998 Russia was on the verge of economic collapse. Now there is a possibility that it could become Europe's top economy by 2030. What can explain such a rapid rise?

OIL AND GAS GIANT

The answer lies under the ground. Russia currently ranks second in the world for oil production, and first for natural gas. Gazprom, a gigantic company which is 50 per cent owned by the Russian state, transports more gas than any other company in the world. International pipelines bring political power, as well as profits. However Vladimir Putin's drive to control business within Russia for his own political purposes, or a failure to deal with corruption, could eventually derail this dash for prosperity.

MINERAL WEALTH

The Russian soil is a treasure chest of other useful resources, such as coal, iron ore, gold, diamonds, chromium, nickel, copper, tin, lead and phosphates. But it can be difficult to mine or drill in Russia's harshest regions and expensive to transport minerals over the huge distances necessary.

WHAT DOES RUSSIA PRODUCE?

Russia's trading partners include China, Japan, the European Union and Turkey. Russia's factories and mills turn out heavy machinery, as well as armaments, aircraft, ships, cars and trucks, chemicals, cotton textiles and household appliances. A high-tech innovations centre, developing projects as varied as biomedical research and space technology, is being developed at Skolvoko, on the outskirts of Moscow.

Workers on the production line at a factory run by the Moscow Brewing Company.

BRICS

Along with Brazil, India, China and South Africa, Russia is part of the BRICS group. These governments want to champion developing economies around the world. All these nations have economies which have been growing very fast. They are all large countries, too, either by area or population (or both). However they all have very different political systems, and this may ultimately make it difficult for them to share economic programmes.

MAKING A LIVING

About 27 per cent of the Russian labour force are industrial workers, and nearly 10 per cent work on the land. The remaining workers provide services, for example as teachers, doctors, cleaners, cooks or office workers. Russia is unusual in having a standard rate of income tax for all, very low at 13 per cent. Some business people make huge fortunes in the new Russia, and there is now a wealthy middle class in Moscow and St Petersburg. However about 1.3 million Russians, many of them working in public services, earn only the national minimum wage. In 2013 this was set at £108 per month, or 5,100 roubles in the national currency. That does not cover the basic costs of living, so many poor people struggle to get by.

Working with wood. Over 20 per cent of the world's forestry resources are found in the Russian Federation.

LIVING IN CITIES

Today seven out of ten Russians live in cities or towns. The biggest cities are Moscow, St Petersburg, Novosibirsk, Yekaterinburg and Nizhny Novgorod.

BEYOND MOSCOW

In a country with such icy winters, it can be very costly to keep roads and housing in more remote towns in good condition. The government plans to tackle this infrastructure problem in the coming years. Too many towns also still depend on just one kind of industry. If a mine or a factory is shut down, there may be no 'plan B' and jobs are less secure today than they were under Soviet rule.

HOUSING OLD AND NEW

City housing reveals just how much everyday life in Russia has changed over the years. In Soviet days all housing was owned by the state. Some people still live in the blocks of single family flats known as *khrushchevki*, because they were constructed when Nikita Khruschev was the Soviet leader, between 1953 and 1964. Built quickly and cheaply, they are short of space and the sitting room generally has to double up as a bedroom by night. Many krushchevki are now being demolished to make room for new homes.

These flats called khrushchevki were built as a temporary answer to Russia's housing shortage and were only designed to last around 35 years.

HOMELESS

St Petersburg – called Leningrad during the Soviet era – is a beautiful city of bridges, canals and rivers. However it shares an ugly problem with many other cities across Russia and around the world – homelessness.

- How many people live in St Petersburg? This is Russia's second largest city, with a population of about 4.8 million.

- How many of them are homeless? Every night over 30,000 people sleep rough on the streets of St Petersburg.

- Why do people have nowhere to go? Some are people with alcohol or drugs problems. Some are former prisoners. Many are children, often orphans. Across the Russian Federation, there may be as many as a million children without a proper home.

- Who helps them? Many charities provide food and temporary shelter.

SPREADING OUT

Town planning is no longer controlled as tightly, so new low-rise developments are growing up in the suburbs, often around metro stations. They in turn encourage more localised businesses, shops and outdoor markets. The most luxurious new apartment blocks in central city districts can only be afforded by the very rich.

Homeless people face a tough existence on the streets of Russia's cities.

Nevsky Prospekt is the main street in St Petersburg. It is always crowded with shoppers and tourists.

19

RURAL RUSSIA

A peaceful summer day in the countryside – but traditional village life is under threat across Russia.

When Russians leave the city streets for a weekend at their dacha, they may be looking for a return to their rural past. Memories of the countryside might include traditional timber houses, dusty farm tracks and the scent of lilac blossom on summer days, or autumn forays into the forest to pick wild mushrooms or bilberries.

VILLAGES AND FARMS

Rural Russia still exists, but it has taken many hard knocks over the years. As cities grow ever more powerful, rural communities are disappearing. Village schools and local hospitals are closing. In 2010 about 3,000 villages were abandoned across Russia. Village life changed greatly in the Soviet era, when family farms were reorganised as part of state-owned farms or collectives. Today another age of change has swept across Russia. Food can be produced on household plots and small peasant farms, or on huge agribusiness estates run by corporations. Farmers from other countries have moved into the Russian market too, buying up land for pig farming or growing crops.

CHERNOZEM COUNTRY

Only about 13 per cent of the Russian Federation is given over to agriculture, because many regions are unsuitable due to climate or soil conditions. The most fertile areas stretch from southwestern Russia into Siberia. They have a rich black soil known as *chernozem*, which is similar to that of the Canadian prairies and is ideal for growing wheat. Barley, oats, rye and maize are also harvested, and root crops include sugarbeet and potatoes. Pigs, cattle and poultry are raised on large and small farms. Large amounts of meat are imported, while cereal exports make Russia the world's fifth largest shipper of wheat. The government is planning greater investment in agriculture in the future.

CLIMATE FUTURES

The future for farming in Russia may depend on climate change. If the climate becomes warmer, as many scientists predict, new areas of the country could become suitable for farming. However in other areas, drought may become more common, making farming very difficult or even turning land into desert.

Wheat stands ripe and ready for the harvest in the Omsk region of southwestern Siberia.

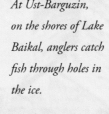

At Ust-Barguzin, on the shores of Lake Baikal, anglers catch fish through holes in the ice.

ACROSS TWO CONTINENTS

The direct distance from Russia's westernmost territory, the Baltic enclave of Kaliningrad, to its easternmost Pacific coast is about 7,700 kilometres. The unity of the world's biggest country, the success of its governance and its economy, all depend on how well the transport system can move people and goods to and fro across this vast section of the planet.

The Trans-Siberian Express railway line links Europe with Asia.

ROAD ROUTES

A network of highways links the cities of European Russia with each other and with Siberia. There are 776,000 kilometres of paved roads in all. Although key routes have been upgraded in recent years, many country roads remain in poor condition and accidents are common.

BY TRAIN

Railways feature in many scenes from classical Russian literature and romantic films, and the Trans-Siberian railway (see below) is famous worldwide. State-owned Russian Railways have the second largest rail network after the USA, with over 87,000 kilometres of track. They carry 1.3 billion passengers a year and a vast amount of freight, from timber to coal. The railways constitute a major economy in themselves, employing about 950,000 people. Ten Russian cities now also have rapid-transit metro or tram networks, either already in service or under construction.

CROSSING RUSSIA

Moscow's Yaroslavsky station is the starting point for one of the world's most awe-inspiring journeys: on board the Trans-Siberian Express. Climb aboard for distant destinations such as the port of Vladivostok on Russia's Pacific coast, or join up with other Siberian networks for links with Ulan Bator in Mongolia, Beijing in China or Pyongyang in North Korea.

- How long is the railway? 9,289 kilometres from Moscow to Vladivostok.

- What is the journey time? It is six days and four hours from Moscow to Vladivostok — and trains generally arrive on time.

BY BOAT

Rivers and canals which are able to carry barges or shipping provide an even bigger transport network than the railways for both passengers and freight. They cross European Russia to link up with the Baltic, the White Sea, the Sea of Azov and the Black Sea. Seaports are very important to a land giant such as Russia, but some Arctic harbours may only be reached with the help of icebreakers. In recent years the decline in summer ice has allowed more ships to travel over the Arctic Ocean.

BY PLANE

Air travel has made the necessity for long and difficult journeys across Russia a thing of the past. Moscow is served by three big airports, with Domodedovo International alone carrying about 22.3 million passengers a year. In all there are 593 airports in Russia and a range of international and internal airlines. The biggest and most profitable of these is Aeroflot, which was founded as the state airline back in 1923.

The Russian ice-breaker 50 Let Pobedy (50 Years of Victory).

ENVIRONMENT AT RISK

The Arctic was once an unspoilt, icy wilderness. No longer. Norilsk in northern Siberia, population 175,000, is one of the coldest cities on the planet – and one of the most polluted, too. It is a centre for mining nickel, and smelting fills the air with a toxic smog. Pollution has affected the health of the people living there. The ground is poisoned with heavy metals and acid rain has destroyed large areas of forest. The mining company Norilsk Nickel says it will cut emissions at Norilsk by about two-thirds between 2015 and 2020, but lasting damage has already been done.

Norilsk produces about 124,000 tonnes of nickel and 304,000 tonnes of copper a year.

PROBLEMS PAST AND PRESENT

Russia's environmental problems have built up over many years. Leaking stocks of old pesticides have polluted land and water. Overgrazing and excessive logging have led to soil erosion. Mining and transport have damaged the tundra. The Barents Sea region of the Arctic has been irradiated by abandoned nuclear submarines and by years of weapons testing during the Cold War.

The Siberian crane is critically endangered.

ENERGY AND CLIMATE

Most scientists blame the release of carbon-based gases from power stations and factories for climate change. The Russian economy relies heavily on carbon-based fuels such as gas, oil and coal, which are used to generate 68 per cent of its electricity. Ten per cent of Russia's energy comes from nuclear fuels, a resource which had a very poor safety record in the old USSR. The 1986 explosion at the Chernobyl power plant (now in independent Ukraine) was probably the world's worst ever nuclear disaster. Scientists also fear that global warming will eventually melt the Siberian permafrost. That could release large amounts of methane into the atmosphere, making the problem of global warming even worse.

A GREEN FUTURE?

Russia does have one renewable energy resource in abundance: water. Hydro-electric power generates 21 per cent of the country's electricity. Other renewables, such as wind and solar power are only now beginning to be developed. The Russian government plans to increase these to make up 4.5 per cent of Russia's energy supply and to introduce other 'green' policies such as energy efficiency and improved recycling, but it has a long way to go.

BEAR NECESSITIES

From tundra and forests to mountains and farmland, Russia is home to a rich variety of wildlife. More brown bears live here than anywhere else on Earth, and they have long been seen as a symbol of the nation. Russia has its wildlife reserves, yet many species are still threatened by the spread of cities, the loss of habitat or prey animals, and widespread hunting.

- Species on the endangered list include the magnificent Siberian tiger, the Amur leopard, the snow leopard, the Russian lynx and the Siberian crane.

- The loss of Arctic sea ice in summer months is a threat to the survival of walruses and polar bears.

FOCUS ON: MOSCOW

MOSCOW METRO

Many of Moscow's commuters travel to work on the underground rail system, or Metro, the third busiest rapid transit system in the word. It has over 300 kilometres of line and is still growing. Some of its stations are very modern, while others dating from the 1930s are built in a lavish, ornate style with statues, fine tiles and chandeliers.

MONEY MAGNET

21st century Moscow is dedicated to making money. An estimated 17 per cent of all Russia's retail sales take place in the capital, and about 20 per cent of Russia's national GDP (gross domestic product, the value of all services and goods) comes from this one city. Moscow's factories produce chemicals, foodstuffs, textiles, cars, aerospace technology, vodka and watches. The head offices of giant energy corporations, such as Gazprom, and new micro-electronic and software companies are also found in Moscow. The city's new central business district is a centre of finance, banking and IT.

PAY

The average Moscow wage is 46,000 roubles (£983) per month, which is about twice as much as the figure for the rest of the country. The minimum legal wage in the city is 12,200 roubles (£260). At the other end of the scale are the city's many billionaires, who enjoy luxury lifestyles.

FINDING WORK

Moscow has the lowest unemployment rate in Russia, so it is hardly surprising that it acts as a magnet for young migrant workers. Many of them are Tajiks, Uzbeks and Kyrgyz from the Central Asian nations that broke away from the old Soviet Union in 1991. They may work as cleaners, snow clearers, builders or market traders. It is a hard life, and for many who work illegally without the proper papers, arrest and deportation is a constant fear.

Built in the Soviet era, Moscow's classic Metro stations were designed to impress the world.

Migrant workers ready for work at a Moscow construction site. Most migrant workers come from the former Soviet Asian republics, such as Turkmenistan.

The GUM building, beside Red Square, is a symbol of Moscow's changing economy. It was a shopping arcade in the 1890s, a Soviet department store in the 1950s and is now a classy shopping mall.

Farmers travel into Moscow to sell fruit and vegetables at the big open air markets.

27

JUSTICE AND THE LAW

Russian justice is often in the headlines. Vladimir Putin repeatedly makes stern calls for law and order. He rejects accusations made by his critics at home, and by international organisations such as the European Parliament, that political pressure is placed on Russian courts of law, or that human rights are being abused.

This is the Moscow headquarters of the Federal Security Service (FSB), which deals with surveillance, border controls and organised crime.

CRIME

Since the 1990s Russia has seen a rise in homicide. Violent crimes are often related to the illegal trafficking of weapons and drugs such as heroin by criminal organisations and gangs. Behind the crime statistics are ongoing social problems, such as poverty, alcoholism and homelessness. Some vulnerable social groups, such as abused women, homosexuals and racial minorities, feel that they are not properly protected either by law or by the justice system.

PUNISHMENT

Most cases go through the district-based People's Courts. Trials are based more upon direct questioning of the accused than on debate between prosecuting and defending lawyers. There is only limited use of juries and acquittals are very rare. The prison regime is very tough. Russia has a high number of prisoners in jail, third only after China and the US. The law allows capital punishment, but nobody has been executed since 1996.

POLICE AND STATE SECURITY

The Russian police used to be called the militia. In 2011 they were renamed, reorganised as a federal force and given a pay rise in a bid to stamp out widespread corruption and improve their public image. State security is the responsibility of the Federal Security Service.

THE DEATH OF SERGEI MAGNITSKY

The strange case of Sergei Magnitsky has highlighted problems in the Russian system of justice.

- **2007** Police raided the Moscow offices of a finance company. They took away documents which later came into the hands of criminals, who used them to transfer ownership of the company to themselves. They then claimed a tax refund of $230 million. Accountant Magnitsky was called in by the finance company to investigate.

- **2008** Magnitsky completed his investigation and filed an official complaint. But then he was arrested instead of the criminals, and accused of tax evasion.

- **2009** Magnitsky was held in prison for nearly a year, interrogated and bullied. He died before going on trial.

- **2010–11** Outrage at the death spread around the world and grew into a full-scale international dispute at government level. After investigations, various officials were removed from their jobs.

- **2012–13** The trial against Magnitsky was re-opened. He was found guilty of fraud. Critics said this was an attempt to intimidate future 'whistleblowers'.

Special police round up 'terrorism suspects' during a 2013 raid on a market in St Petersburg.

RIGHTS – OR WRONGS?

The conflict between government authority and human rights has a long history in Russia, as in many other parts of the world. Both Tsarist and Soviet rulers were authoritarian and operated secret police forces. Today there are still concerns that political opponents of the government or 'whistleblowers' who expose corruption or crime may be targeted or killed by criminals, security agents or police.

KNOWLEDGE AND HEALTH

1st September is 'Knowledge Day' in Russia – the first day of the new school year. Children bring flowers for the teacher. They face four terms in the coming year, with school starting each day at 8.00 am and ending about 2pm. Education has long been highly valued in Russia, and 99.6 per cent of the adult population can read and write.

GOING TO SCHOOL

Russian schooling demands 11 years of compulsory education, with four spent in primary, five in secondary and two in high. Often all three levels are housed in the same building. Some children also go to pre-school classes, before the age of six. Free education is provided by the state, although since the 1990s private schools have also been introduced for those who can afford to pay the fees.

Another year means a fresh start at this Moscow school, marked by bouquets for the teachers.

COLLEGE SHAKE-UP

Higher education includes vocational training colleges and universities. Private colleges are now permitted to take students as well. After the Soviet era, more and more teenagers wanted to go on to college. The number of universities grew rapidly, but at the same time standards began to slide. In 2013 a new programme was introduced of closing down failing colleges and channelling funds to the top performers. Improving scientific research is a priority.

Lomonosov Moscow State University is the oldest and largest college in Russia.

HEALTH ISSUES

In the 1950s, Russians could expect to live longer than Americans, but in the 1990s their life expectancy fell dramatically, as the Soviet social welfare system was cut drastically. Today life expectancy is creeping up again, at 76 for women and 64 for men. The sharp difference between the two sexes has been put down to drinking habits. Life expectancy is still low when compared with 82 for women and 78 for men in the UK. Major health risks include cancer and heart disease from smoking, and damage to the liver and heart caused by alcohol abuse.

MEDICINE IN RUSSIA

National healthcare is partly funded by compulsory insurance schemes and partly by the taxpayer. Private treatment is now available too. Russia has a very high proportion of doctors and hospital beds to the population, but the organisation of healthcare has been poor and government funding has lagged far behind the countries of the West. Putin's government is now putting serious investment into healthcare and modernising the service, but it will take some years for things to improve.

A Russian nurse holds a newborn baby. Russia today has a very low rate of population growth.

MEDIA MESSAGES

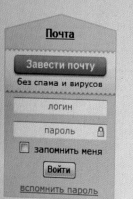
The Yandex search engine is the most popular in Russia, with a 64 per cent share of the market.

Russia is part of the digital revolution which has swept the world. Telecommunications and information technology have had a great effect on the BRICS countries, bypassing many of the problems associated with poor infrastructure and long-distance communication. Russia has 44 million landline telephones and about 102 million mobiles, of which smartphones make up 37 percent.

ONLINE IN RUSSIA

There are about 70 million Internet users in Russia and eight in ten of them log on to social networking sites. Russian-based sites such as VK and Odnoklassiki are very popular with Russian speakers both in Russia and abroad. The top search engine is run by another Russian company, Yandex.

CENSORSHIP

From 2011 to 2013 the Internet has been widely used to organise and coordinate protests about disputed election results and against government policies said to be authoritarian. However Russia, unlike China, has not attempted to seal off international political influence with a firewall. New laws passed in 2012 do blacklist certain sites if they are believed to promote social problems such as drug abuse, and these laws were used to shut down, briefly, a satirical Russian website called Lurkmore.

A FREE PRESS?

While the traditional press is in decline in many Western countries, Russian newspapers can still boast a yearly circulation of about 8.2 billion copies. Russia has more journalists than any other country in the world. There is little formal censorship, but the government will brief, bribe and intimidate the press to get a story across. Journalists who investigate criminal activity or corruption have risked being attacked or murdered. One was the writer Anna Politovskaya, shot dead outside her flat by unknown persons in 2006. She had uncovered breaches of human rights during the conflict in Chechnya and was a fearless critic of Vladimir Putin.

A newspaper and magazine kiosk shows the variety of publications for sale in Russia.

The recording studio of a very popular Russian TV talent show called KVN.

TV REALITY

Russia is a nation of avid television viewers. Comedies, crime thrillers, game and reality shows win big audiences. There are six federal television channels and many more regional and local broadcasters, as well as hundreds of radio stations. A state-funded multi-language international television network called Russia Today (RT) has been very successful, attracting a worldwide audience of 550 million people. About two-thirds of all media are owned or part-owned by the state. Most political programmes play it safe, and many younger people have deserted the mainstream media for Internet viewing.

ARTS, MUSIC AND SPORTS

An international ballet festival is staged at Moscow's famous Bolshoi Theatre.

Russia's peoples have a long tradition of costume and embroidery, of decoration and woodcarving, of playing musical instruments such as the three-stringed balalaika, of energetic folk dances. When it comes to fine painting, music, dance, literature and cinema, Russia has an extraordinary record.

RUSSIAN GENIUS

Russia's artistic tradition dates back to the richly ornamented religious icons of the Middle Ages. The 18th century saw the founding of classical ballet companies such as the Mariinsky and the Bolshoi, and the start of one of the world's great art collections at the Hermitage museum in St Petersburg. The 19th century was a golden era for Russian culture. There were the stirring symphonies and concertos of the great composer Pyotr Ilyich Tchaikovsky. Great writers such as Fyodor Dostoyevsky and Leo Tolstoy introduced Russia to the world. The turbulent twentieth century saw yet more artistic creativity, from the films of Sergei Eisenstein to the music of Sergei Prokofiev and Dmitri Shostakovich.

PRANKS AND PUNKS

Since the fall of the Soviet Union, Russian artists and musicians have been finding new directions, testing out the new nature of political power and wealth, and using installations, video and other new media to get their message across. Satire, shock and rebellion have been common themes. Crazed perfomance art from Oleg Kulik caught international attention, as did a feminist punk band called Pussy Riot. In 2012 they outraged the Russian authorities by performing their 'Punk Prayer: Mother of God Chase Putin Away' in Moscow's Cathedral of Christ the Saviour. Accused of religious hatred, they were sentenced to two years in a prison camp. In May 2013 one member, Maria Alyokhina, went on hunger strike when she was refused parole.

Out to shock... feminist punk band Pussy Riot perform in Moscow.

TIME OUT

To many Russians, performance does not mean theatre or ballet, but how well their favourite team is doing. Football is the most popular spectator sport. There is huge interest in the national team and the 2018 FIFA World Cup will be hosted by Russia. In recent years, as elsewhere, the game's fortunes have depended upon backing from billionaires, who can propel minor clubs like FC Anzhi Makhachkala to international fame with big international signings. Other top sports in Russia are ice hockey and basketball.

Russia's national ice hockey team takes on Canada at a world championsip contest.

RELIGION AND CUSTOMS

Christianity came to the Slavs from Constantinople (modern Istanbul) over 1,100 years ago, and was a cornerstone of the Russian state under the tsars. However Soviet communism was officially atheist. It was hostile to all religions, dismissing them as superstitions used by the powerful to hold back social progress. Many churches were destroyed or taken over. Although religions were not banned, in practice believers were often persecuted or sent to labour camps.

OLD WAYS

Many Russians remain atheists today, but the Russian Orthodox Church is thriving again, supported by around 40 per cent of the population. Major churches in the big cities have been rebuilt or restored, although many rural churches remain in a dilapidated state. Controversially the leaders of the Russian Orthodox Church are as close to Putin as they were to the tsars in the old days. The Church tends towards being pro-government, nationalist and conservative. Religious education has been made a compulsory part of the school curriculum. Some Russians are members of other Christian churches and sects.

A Russian Orthodox wedding ceremony. The candles represent the light of Christ, while crowns mark the union of man and woman.

One of the largest mosques in Russia is at the heart of Grozny, in Chechnya.

MULTI-FAITH

Nearly seven per cent of all Russians are Muslims. Most of them live in the Caucasus mountains and in the Central Asian regions of the federation. Jews once played a major role in Russian society, but over the centuries many of them fled persecution in Russia to settle elsewhere in Europe or in the United States. From the 1970s and 80s onwards, many emigrated to Israel. Many remaining Jews are secular rather than religious. Buddhism has followers in some southern regions. In recent years there has been a revival of interest in pagan beliefs held by the Slavs and by peoples of Siberia in ancient times.

FESTIVALS AND FEASTS

- Christmas Day is celebrated on 7th January.

- Malenitsa is celebrated in the seventh week before Easter. Pancakes are made and there are sleigh rides, snowball fights and the burning of a straw effigy.

- Real eggs, hand-painted in beautiful patterns and colours, are exchanged at Easter. Food treats include a round cheesecake with fruits and almonds, known as Pashka (which is the same as the word for Easter).

- St Petersburg is so far north that it barely gets dark at night around midsummer. These 'White Nights' are celebrated with music, dancing and boat rides.

FOCUS ON: MOSCOW

ENJOYING THE CITY

How do Muscovites relax? On a hot summer's day they may take a boat ride on the Moscow River. Many go swimming in the water, despite the pollution. Some even swim there on freezing days in the winter, but more sensible people just fish – through holes bored in the ice.

MEETING PLACES

In 2011 Moscow's Gorky Park, a former funfair site, was redeveloped to become a fashionable meeting place, offering ice skating, salsa dancing classes and an open-air cinema. Other city parks and green spaces are also being refurbished. Moscow's *banyas* (bath-houses) are traditional saunas where you can luxuriate in steam before being beaten with a branch of oak leaves! Men and women have separate areas where they can meet up to socialise and have a drink.

ENTERTAINMENT

The Old Moscow Circus opened on Tsvetnoy Boulevard in 1880 and its clowns have continued to entertain the public ever since. Moscow's theatres offer opera, classic drama and the world-famous Bolshoi ballet. Sports fans are fortunate in Moscow, which has five of Russia's top football teams – Spartak, Lokomotiv, CSKA, FC Moscow and Dynamo. The city is also home to the Luzhniki national stadium.

FOOD AND CELEBRATION

The growing wealth in the city has changed Muscovites' attitude to eating. Many now attend food festivals or dine out at fancy restaurants run by celebrity chefs. Every sort of international cuisine is available in the city these days. Traditional Russian cooking is also delicious, with dishes such as *borscht* (beetroot soup), *shchi* (cabbage soup), beef Stroganoff (sautéed strips of meat served with soured cream), Moscow chicken (creamy, served with onions and mushrooms called cepes), *blinis* (thin pancakes), and *pirozhki* (glazed buns with fillings such as mushroom, egg, beef, salmon or fruit). Family gatherings, weddings and anniversaries bring out the Muscovites' love of celebration, with hours of feasting, drinking, dancing, intense conversation and discussion around the dining tables.

Moscow's classiest banya, the Sanduny, dates back to 1808 and has been restored to its original splendour. It includes a magnificent swimming pool.

The grand Pushkin Museum of Fine Arts shows European masterpieces, while the State Tretyakov Gallery houses the nation's most important collection of Russian paintings.

Hunting for a bargain? The bustling Izmailovo market offers cheap clothing, handicrafts, antiques, souvenirs such as Russian dolls or samovars (traditional urns for making tea) and street snacks such as kebabs and samosas.

Skaters take to the ice in Moscow's Gorky Park, recently re-styled as a fashionable recreation centre.

Black caviar is made up of the eggs from a fish called the sturgeon and can be served with a blini and a glass of champagne – a very expensive delicacy!

RUSSIA INTERNATIONAL

Tourists now flock to see Russia's historic buildings, such as the Hermitage in St Petersburg.

Today's generation of politicians grew up in the days of the Cold War. In those days people in the West used to say that Russia was 'behind the Iron Curtain', meaning that it was cut off from the rest of the world.

BRAVE NEW WORLD

Today all that has changed. Western tourists and business people move freely about the streets of Moscow and St Petersburg and enjoy themselves. Ordinary Russians now travel abroad as holidaymakers. Moscow's super-rich invest overseas, in property, football clubs and media. These days it is Russia's pipelines and wealth, rather than its military power, which has made it a big player in international politics.

A GAME OF CHESS

Cold War attitudes do still linger, on both sides. Putin and his prime minister, Medvedev, are always quick to defend what they see as Russia's national interests. In 2012 Russia spoke out against US plans to install a missile defence system in Poland, which Russia regarded as a threat to its security. In recent years Russia's relations with Iran and Syria, a former ally, have also worried Western governments. Russia's record on human rights is another recurring issue in international politics. The death in prison of whistleblower Sergei Magnitsky in 2009 (see p.29) has triggered an ongoing dispute between Russia and the United States.

THE FUTURE

Closer contact and a great deal of genuine cooperation between the United States, the European Union and Russia have already made the world a much safer place. As part of BRICS, Russia has also been building bridges in Asia, Africa and South America.

So is Russia misrepresented in the Western media and unfairly criticised? Many Russians believe so. It is certainly true that human rights abuses, severe environmental problems, corruption, or the gap between the richest and poorest in society, are not unique to Russia. They are in the news all over the world and may be applied to some of Russia's critics. But in whichever country these problems arise, they have to be dealt with for the sake of a future which actually works. And there is no shortage of young Russians who are ready to take up that challenge.

US President Barack Obama and Dimitry Medvedev shake hands. The relations between the two world powers have improved greatly since the Cold War, but tensions remain.

WHICH WAY FORWARD?

The English statesman Winston Churchill said in 1939 that Russia was 'a riddle, wrapped in a mystery, wrapped in an enigma'. His phrase reminds us of one of those Russian matryoshka dolls, in which each doll contains smaller models of itself. You often see them on sale painted in the likeness of Russia's leaders, present to past, one inside the other.

RUSSIA'S MANY COLOURS

The multi-layered nature of the new Russia can be seen at parades and demonstrations in the cities. Here is the national red, white and blue tricolour. There is the flag of the USSR, red for revolution with a hammer-and-sickle emblem representing the workers. Here too are the black, gold and white flags of the nineteenth century empire, flown by royalists and ultra-nationalists. There are also the white ribbons widely worn by opponents of Vladimir Putin.

PAST LESSONS?

Putin urges his followers to be inspired by Russian history, but that raises many conflicting ideas. The motto of Tsar Nicholas II was 'Orthodoxy, autocracy and nationality'. The Communist leader Lenin said, 'Freedom in capitalist society always remains...Freedom for slave owners.' Reformer Gorbachev called for 'Restructuring and Openness'. Today's school leavers, preparing to vote for the first time, are faced by many decisions if they are to decide the best way forward.

A nest of matryoshka dolls represents Russian leaders (left to right): Nikita Khrushchev, Leonid Brezhnev, Mikhail Gorbachev, Boris Yelstsin, Dimitry Medvedev and Vladimir Putin.

After the 'Last Bell' ceremony, high school graduates head out to have some fun. What will the future hold for them?

VOTING FOR HOPE

In a way they are fortunate. Russia has great economic potential if it is managed wisely. Its people are tough, having learned how to endure a harsh climate and adapt to a challenging landscape. They have survived authoritarian rule and fought off invasions. Their writers and musicians have inspired the world. They live in the largest country on the planet and, if its landscape can be preserved, one of awe-inspiring beauty.

A symbol of old Russia, the 12th century Church of the Intercession rises from the banks of the River Neri.

GLOSSARY

acid rain Acidic rainfall, polluted by sulphur dioxide or nitrogen oxides.

acquittal Being found not guilty of a crime.

ally A country which is on the same side as another.

armaments Weapons of war.

atheist Not believing in a god or gods.

autocracy Rule by a monarch or leader with absolute power.

authoritarian Demanding loyalty to the government above individual freedom.

balalaika A three-stringed musical instrument with a triangular body.

Bolsheviks Members of a faction in the Russian Social Democratic Labour Party, which seized power in the October Revolution of 1917. This later became the Communist Party of the Soviet Union.

BRICS A grouping of nations with rapidly developing economies – Brazil, Russia, India, China and South Africa.

capital punishment The death penalty.

capitalism An economic system based on private ownership and the accumulation of wealth.

civil war A war fought between people from the same country.

circulation Of a newspaper or magazine, the number of copies distributed.

climate change A major change in weather patterns and conditions measured over a long period.

Cold War A period of great international tension between the United States and its allies on one side, and communist countries such as the Soviet Union and China on the other.

collective A working enterprise shared by a number of people or groups.

communism A political system based upon rule by a political party representing the working class.

conservative Supporting tradition, opposing change.

corruption Dishonest practice, such as bribery of officials.

Cyrillic A system of writing based on Greek letters, which evolved into the Russian alphabet.

elite A small group of powerful, wealthy or talented people.

emissions Gases or other substances given out by a process, such as pollution from a power station.

enclave A territory of one country which is surrounded by the lands of another.

erosion The wearing down of soil or rock by wind, water, ice or heat.

ethnic group A group of people sharing ancestry, customs and culture.

faction A group of people with shared political aims, often within a larger political grouping.

federal Representing the Russian Federation as a whole, rather than individual regions or cities.

firewall Computer hardware or software designed to isolate a network and control its traffic.

GDP Gross Domestic Product, the value of goods and services produced within a country over a given period of time.

global warming A long term rise in the Earth's temperature.

head of state The senior person representing a nation, such as a president or a monarch.

heavy metals A term often used to describe toxic metals which cause pollution.

homicide The killing of another human being.

human rights The basic conditions required to ensure life, liberty and justice.

hydroelectric Power derived from turbines driven by water.

icebreaker A ship specially designed to force its way through frozen sea.

icon A religious painting produced as an act of devotion.

infrastructure Basic systems such as roads, drainage, water and electricity mains, transport and communications.

irradiate To contaminate with radioactive material.

life expectancy The average period one can expect to live.

methane A chemical compound found in natural gas.

militia A citizen fighting force, formerly the name of the police in Russia.

minimum wage The lowest wage that can be legally paid in a country or region.

minority An ethnic group or class of people who make up less than half the total population.

missile defence A system designed to attack or prevent incoming enemy missiles.

oligarch A member of a ruling elite, or in modern Russia any individual with great power and wealth.

Pacific rim The lands bordering the Pacific Ocean.

pagan Pre-Christian religions related to nature and the countryside.

peasant A poor rural worker.

permafrost In Arctic lands, a layer of soil that remain frozen all year round.

population density The number of people living within a given unit of area.

renewable Any form of energy that comes from a source that is continually replenished, such as wind or the Sun, and not from finite resources such as coal, oil or uranium.

republic In Russia, an administrative division in which there is a high proportion of non-ethnic Russians.

sect A religious grouping or faction.

secular Non-religious

serf A labourer who has to work the land for his master and has no right to move away or seek other employment.

smelt To obtain metal by heating ore in a furnace.

steppe Grassland or prairie.

taiga A northern forest environment dominated by pines, spruces and larches.

tricolour A flag made up of three bands of colour.

tsar A Russian emperor.

tundra Treeless plains and mountains bordering the polar regions.

Turkic An ethnic group or language originating in Central Asia.

ultra-nationalist Someone who believes in the superiority of their nation.

FURTHER INFORMATION

BOOKS

Countries Around the World: Russia, Jilly Hunt (Raintree, 2012)

Countries in Our World: Russia, Galya Ransome (Franklin Watts, 2012)

WEBSITES

http://www.bbc.co.uk/news/world-europe-17840446
BBC's Russia profile and timeline.

http://russiapedia.rt.com/basic-facts-about-russia/
Russia Today's 'Russiapedia', a useful summary of Russia today.

http://www.spartacus.schoolnet.co.uk/Russia.htm
Access to a wide-ranging series of articles and profiles from Russian history.

http://travel.nationalgeographic.co.uk/travel/countries/russia-guide/
National Geographic's views of travel through Russia

INDEX